THE VISUAL DRUMSET METHOD

T0066671

To access audio visit:
www.halleonard.com/mylibrary

Enter Code
5554-3504-8058-3760

ISBN 978-1-4234-9523-9

HAL•LEONARD®
CORPORATION

7777 W. BLUEMOUND RD. P.O. BOX 13819 MILWAUKEE, WI 53213

In Australia Contact:
Hal Leonard Australia Pty. Ltd.
4 Lentara Court
Cheltenham, Victoria, 3192 Australia
Email: ausadmin@halleonard.com.au

Visit Hal Leonard Online at
www.halleonard.com

DEDICATION

I would like to dedicate
this book to
my son Aaron
and my wife Joy.

CREDITS

JOHN FINK — electric guitar tracks

TIM ADRIANSON — bass guitar tracks

MATTHEW ADRIANSON — original
songs, drums/keyboard/percussion
tracks, mixing and mastering

CONTENTS

PREFACE

The concept behind this book was to use pictures instead of normal music notation to communicate how to play basic drum beats. In teaching both piano and drums privately, I've found that students learn in different ways. You might have to communicate the same idea multiple ways before one of them clicks with any given student. In a world of multimedia including video games, why not make learning drum beats more visual? In hopes of making learning less intimidating and more fun, I have constructed a visual approach using pictures and audio tracks. If you don't have a drumset, use the cutout sheet on page 31 and place the pictures of the hi-hat and snare drum on a table, and the picture of the bass drum on the floor. You do not need to cross the right hand over the left hand if you are using the picture cutout sheet. Simply place the hi-hat cutout on your right and the snare drum cutout on your left. Use the picture cutouts to follow along with the audio tracks. On the audio tracks each exercise and drum beat is played eight times. The beginning

exercises cover striking each instrument separately and all combinations of instruments used in this book. Once you can play the exercises, you have the tools you need to play all of the drum beats that follow. Above each exercise and drum beat you will see "1 & 2 & 3 & 4 & ." This is a traditional way of counting and is helpful for keeping track of where you are. Practice with each track as many times as needed. Once you feel comfortable playing a given drum beat, try playing that beat along with any of the songs starting on track 49. Each song first has a track with drums and then a track without drums. The goal is to get used to playing with other instruments. The audio tracks for the beginning exercises are at 30 beats per minute, and the drum beats are at 52 beats per minute. If you are wondering what that means, there are 60 seconds in a minute, so 60 beats per minute is one beat per second. A metronome and the song tracks will help you practice these drum beats at tempos other than 52 beats per minute.

TECHNIQUE
Right-Hand Grip

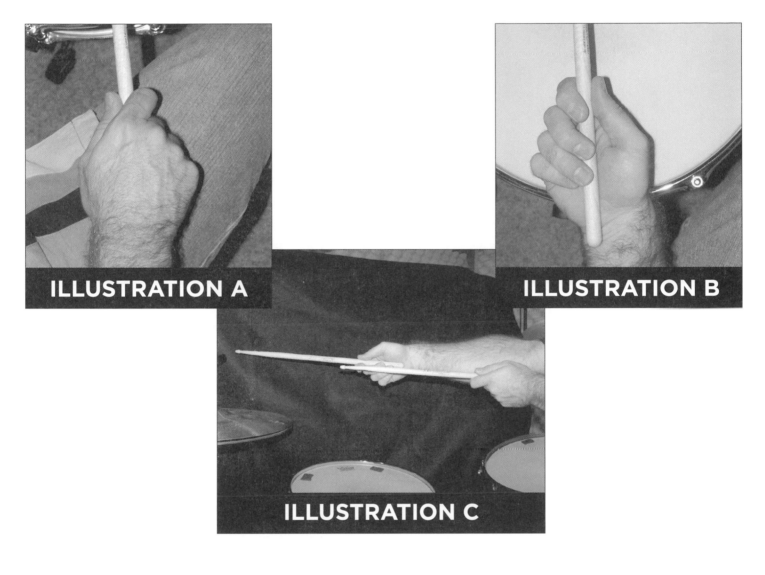

ILLUSTRATION A

ILLUSTRATION B

ILLUSTRATION C

The right-hand grip is made up of two components. The first component, shown in illustration A, consists of your thumb and your pointer finger. The flat part of your thumb goes on the side of the stick and points down the stick. Your pointer finger wraps around the stick, touching it underneath. The second component, shown in illustration B, consists of your other three fingers on the underside of the stick. As you can see in illustration B your middle finger and ring finger are touching the stick, and your pinky is tucked right next to your ring finger. Think of the stick going through the middle of your hand, which when turned over will create a straight line from your elbow to the tip of the stick. Your grip should not be tight. You need to hold onto the stick just enough that it doesn't fall out of your hand. When you strike a cymbal or drum you will tighten your grip a little more.

Left-Hand Grip

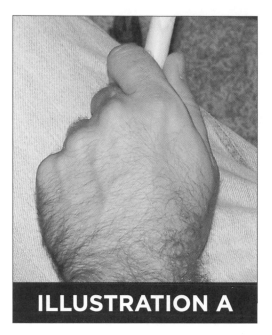

ILLUSTRATION A

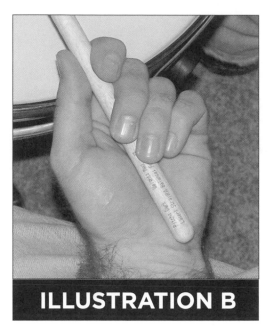

ILLUSTRATION B

The left-hand grip is a mirror image of the right-hand grip. The first component of the left-hand grip, shown in illustration A, consists of your thumb and your pointer finger. The flat part of your thumb goes on the side of the stick and is pointing down the stick. Your pointer finger is wrapped around the stick. The second component of the grip is your other three fingers on the underside of the stick. As you can see in illustration B, your middle finger and ring finger are touching the stick, and your pinky is tucked right next to your ring finger.

Playing Position

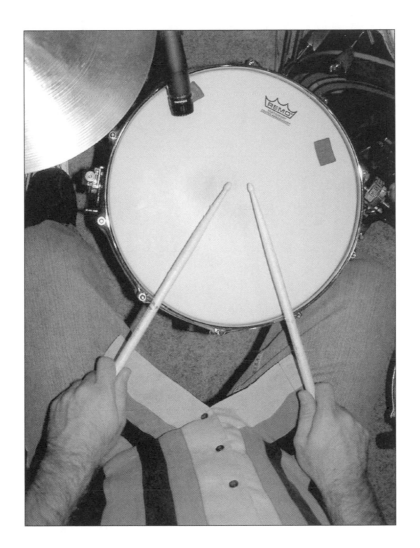

Playing position on the snare drum is a good place to get familiar with holding the sticks and striking the drum. The grip and technique for striking the snare drum will hold true when moving around the drumset. In playing position both tips of your sticks are in the center of the snare drum. They are approximately at a 45 degree angle. You could think of playing position as looking like an "A" or an upside down "V." Think of each stick as an extension of your arm and hand. You should be able to draw a straight line from each of your elbows to the tips of your sticks. The tops of your hands should be flat. Think of holding handlebars on a bike. Your elbows should be relaxed at your sides, and you should sit up straight. Good posture is important and will help you play better.

Right Foot and Right Leg Position

Your right foot should be over the bass drum pedal with your heel off the foot board. The main point of contact should be the ball of your foot.

When striking the bass drum, the beater will go into the head, but allow it to come back off the head after impact.

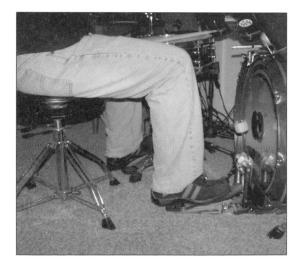

Think of your leg as being straight over the bass drum pedal. This will allow you to use your leg for both power and speed.

Striking a Snare Drum

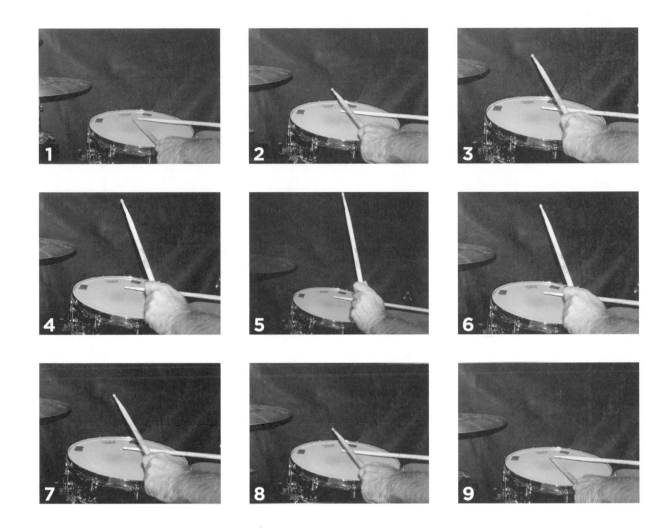

The basics of striking the snare drum involve a two-part motion. Starting at playing position, with your sticks about one inch above the drumhead, the stroke is up and then down. After striking the drum your stick should return to playing position. Don't leave the stick on the drumhead. Remember to relax, and the force of striking the drum will naturally bring the stick back off the head. Two points of focus are your wrist and the tip of your stick. Your wrist will bend up during the up motion and bend down during the down motion. The tip of your stick also goes up and down beginning and ending about an inch off the drumhead. Notice the progression of the tip of the drumstick and the wrist in the photos above. When playing more aggressively you may also bend at your elbow and use your arm. For the first time through the drum beats in this book, we will focus on bending at the wrist. Exaggerate the motion to make sure that you are really bending your wrist.

Striking the Hi-Hat

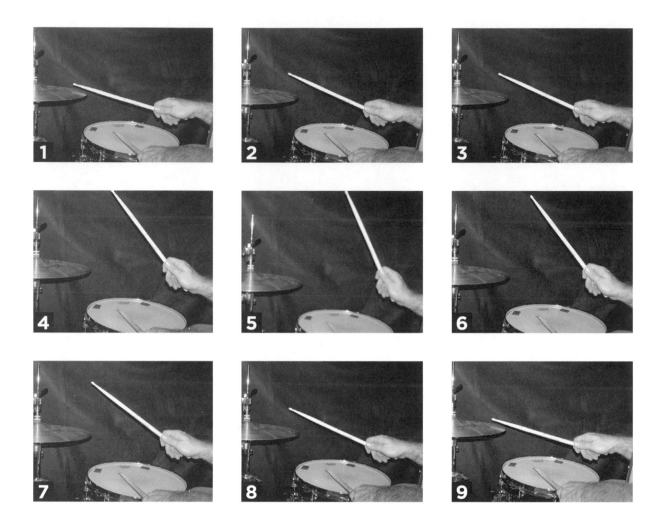

As with the snare drum, striking the hi-hat is a two-part motion. While maintaining playing position with your left hand, move your right hand/stick over to the hi-hat as shown above. Don't leave the stick on the hi-hat. Remember to relax, and the force of striking the hi-hat will naturally bring the stick back off the hi-hat. Two points of focus are your wrist and the tip of your stick. Your wrist will bend up during the up motion and bend down during the down mo-tion. The tip of your stick also goes up and down beginning and ending about an inch off the hi-hat. Notice the progression of the tip of the drumstick and the wrist in the photos above. When playing more aggressively you may also bend at your elbow and use your arm. While learning the drum beats in this book, we will focus on bending at the wrist. Exaggerate the motion to make sure that you are really bending your wrist.

AUDIO TRACKS

BEGINNING EXERCISES	TRACK
Hi-Hat Only	1
Snare Drum Only	2
Bass Drum Only	3
Hi-Hat and Snare Drum	4
Hi-Hat and Bass Drum	5
Hi-Hat, Snare Drum, and Bass Drum	6
Drum Beats	7–48
Song Tracks	49–58

DRUM KEY

 HI-HAT / RIGHT HAND

SNARE DRUM / LEFT HAND

 BASS DRUM / RIGHT FOOT

Your right hand/stick plays the hi-hat, your left hand/stick plays the snare drum, and your right foot plays the bass drum.

BEGINNING EXERCISES

HI-HAT ONLY

TRACK
1

| 1 | & | . | 2 | & | 3 | & | 4 | & |

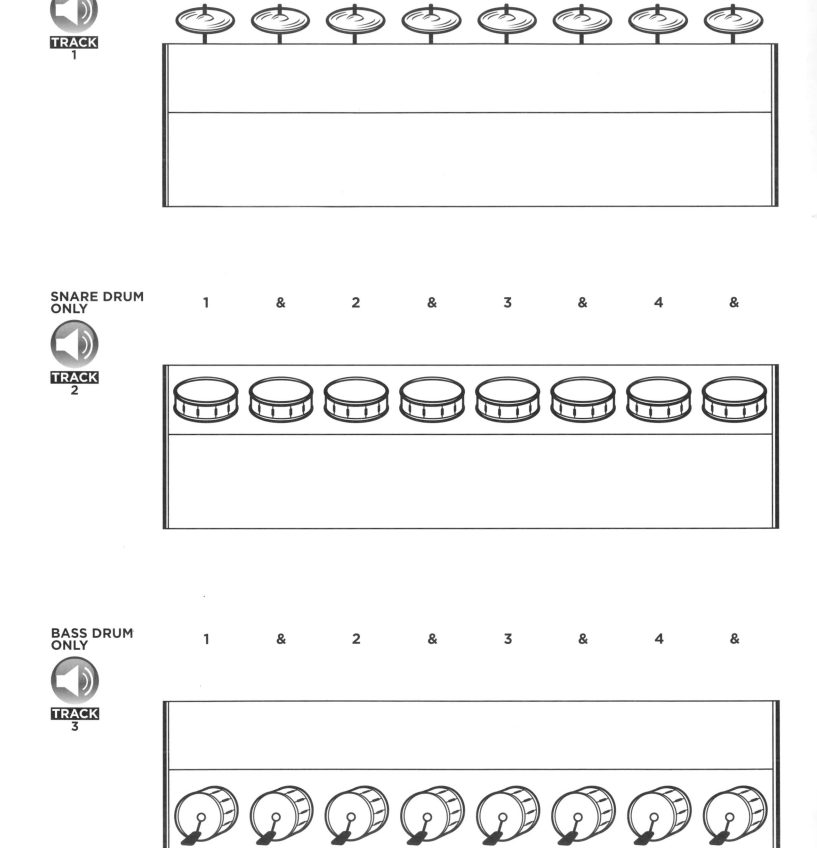

SNARE DRUM ONLY

TRACK
2

| 1 | & | 2 | & | 3 | & | 4 | & |

BASS DRUM ONLY

TRACK
3

| 1 | & | 2 | & | 3 | & | 4 | & |

HI-HAT AND SNARE DRUM

TRACK 4

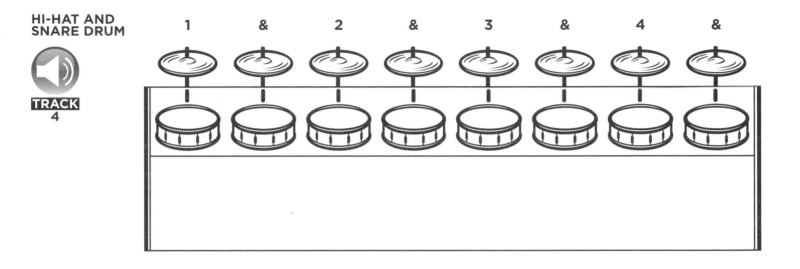

HI-HAT AND BASS DRUM

TRACK 5

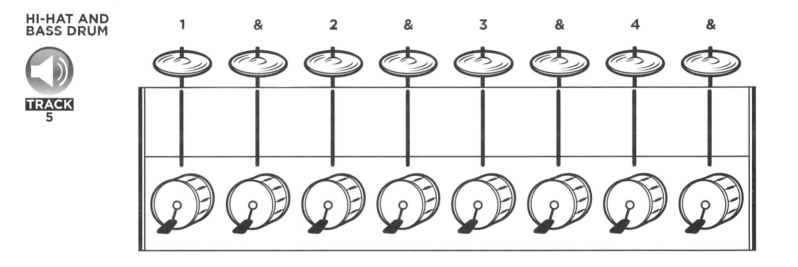

HI-HAT, SNARE DRUM, AND BASS DRUM

TRACK 6

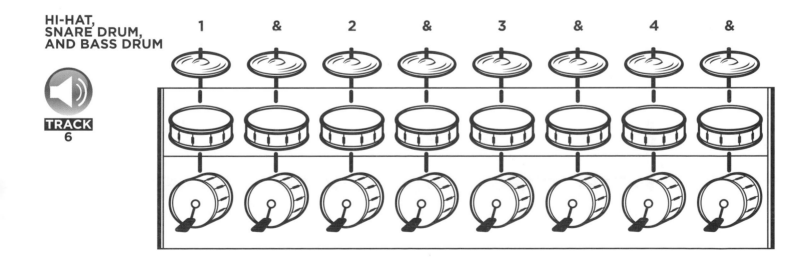

DRUM BEATS

Try practicing beats 1 through 6 with song tracks 49 and 50 on the audio.

1	&	2	&	3	&	4	&

1)

TRACK 7

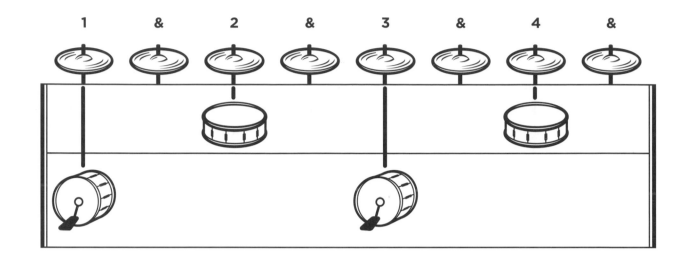

1	&	2	&	3	&	4	&

2)

TRACK 8

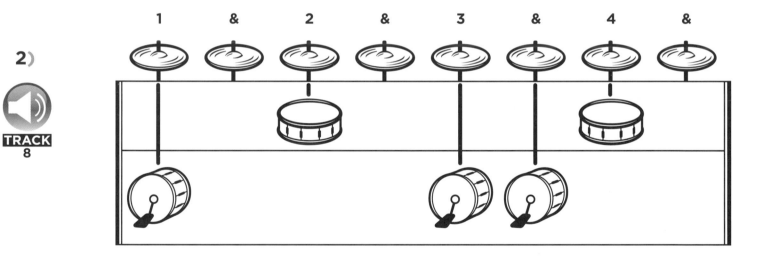

1	&	2	&	3	&	4	&

3)

TRACK 9

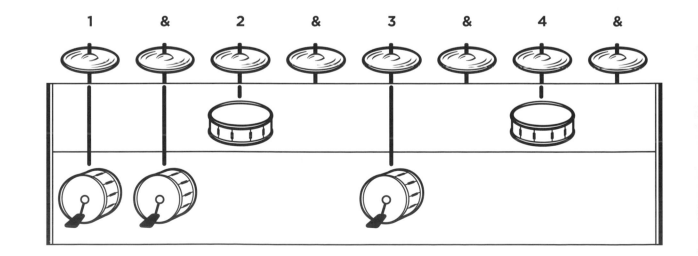

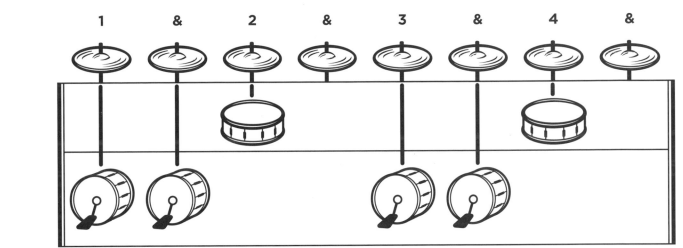

TRACK
11

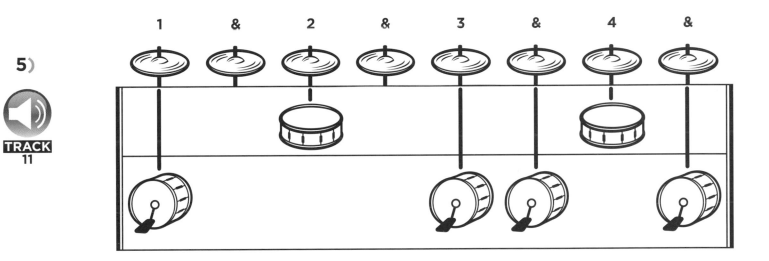

TRACK
12

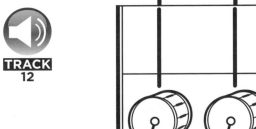

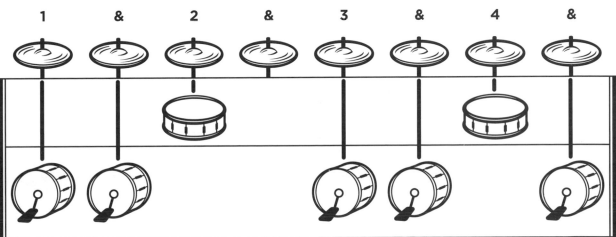

Try practicing beats 7 through 12 with song tracks 51 and 52.

7)

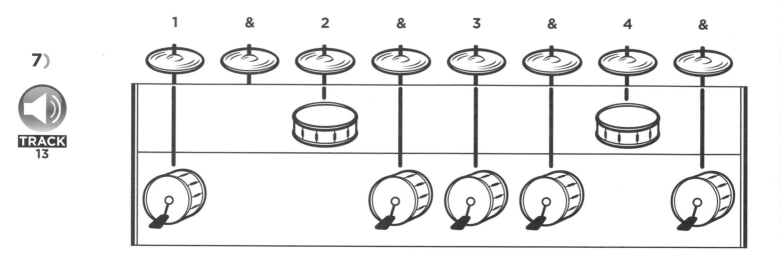

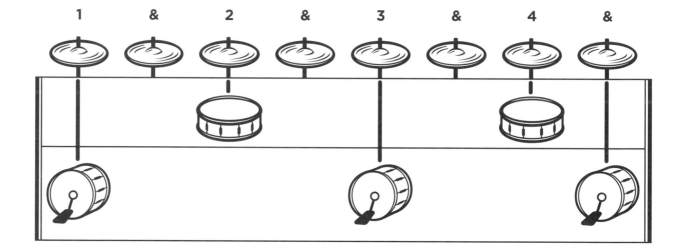

8)

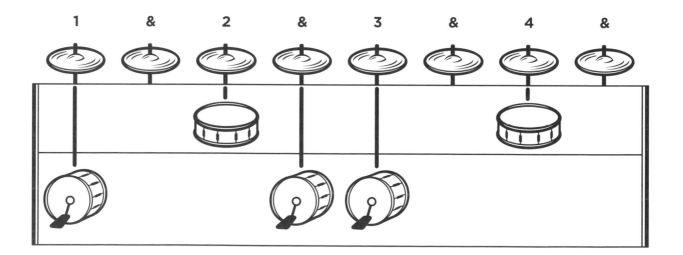

9)

10) TRACK 16

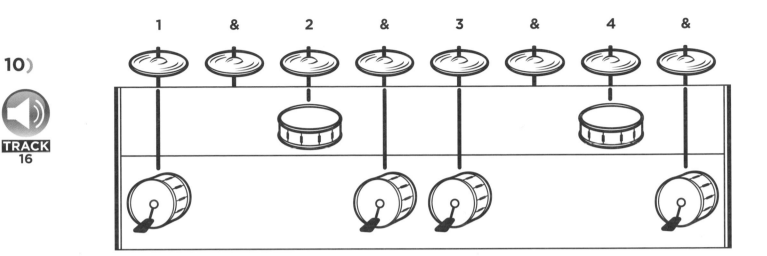

11)  TRACK 17

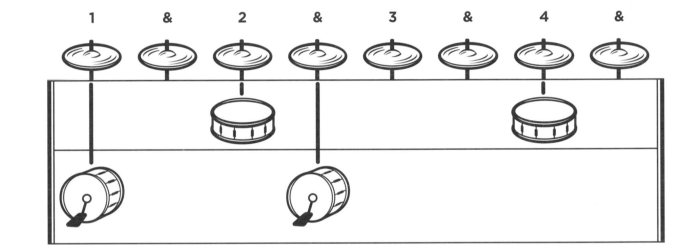

12) TRACK 18

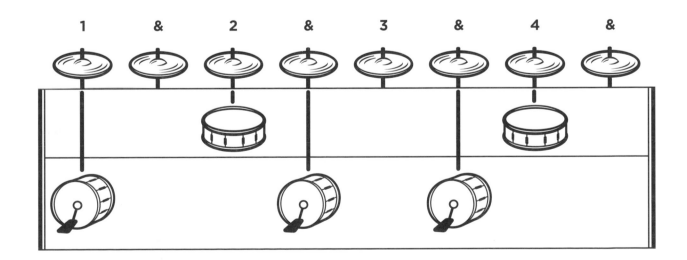

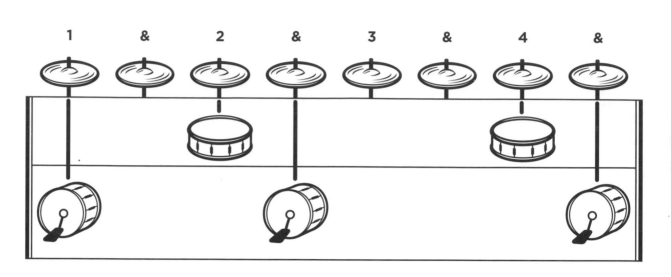

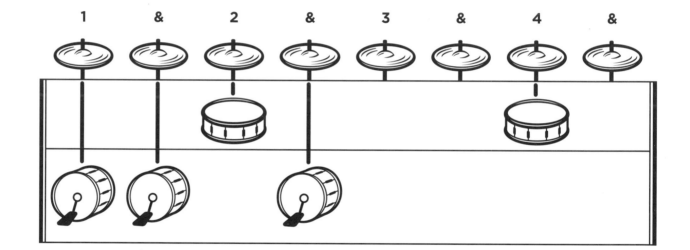

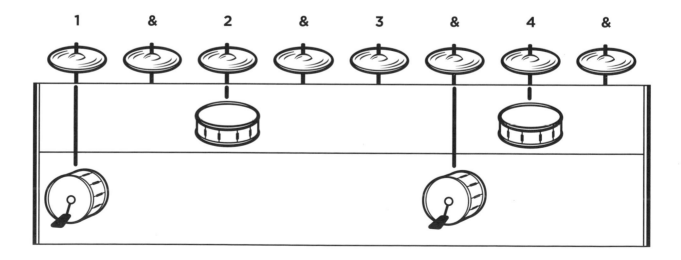

TRACK
22

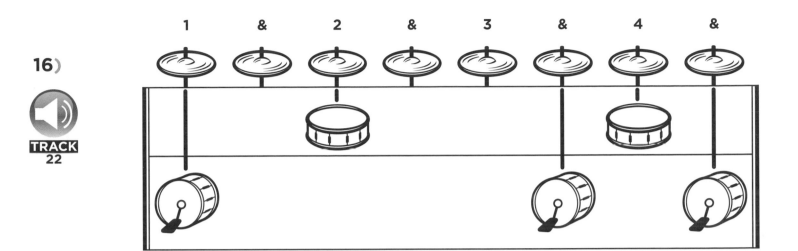

17)

TRACK
23

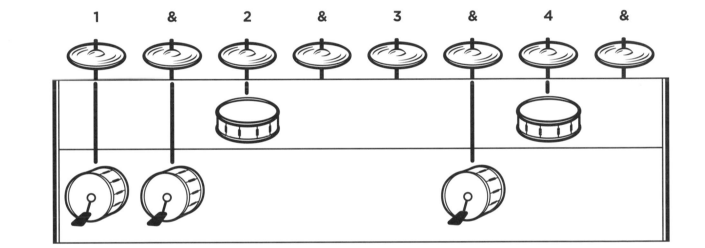

18)

TRACK
24

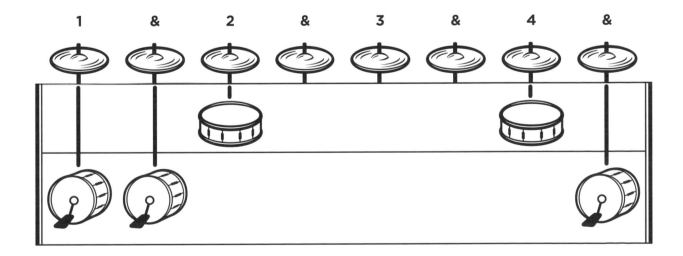

19)

TRACK 25

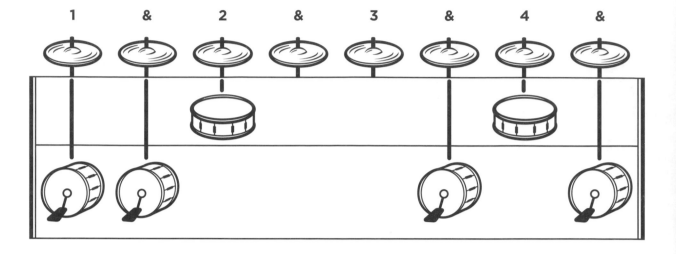

20)

TRACK 26

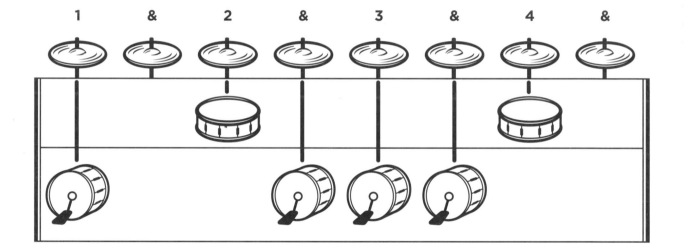

21)

TRACK 27

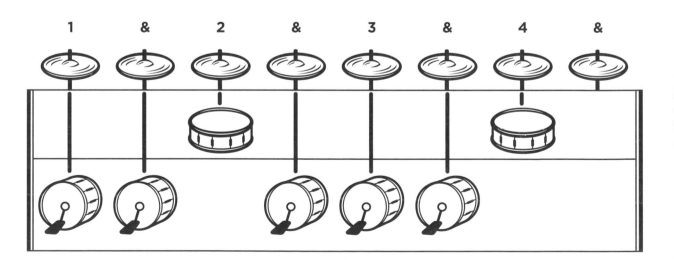

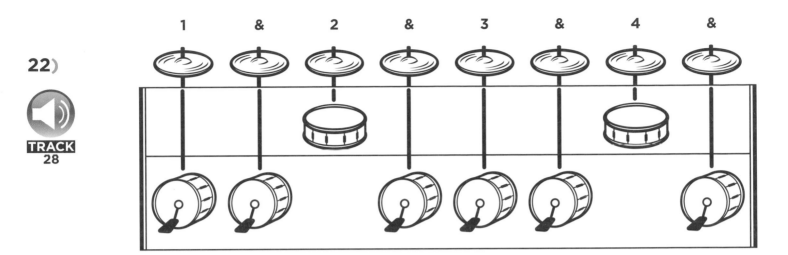

23)

TRACK
29

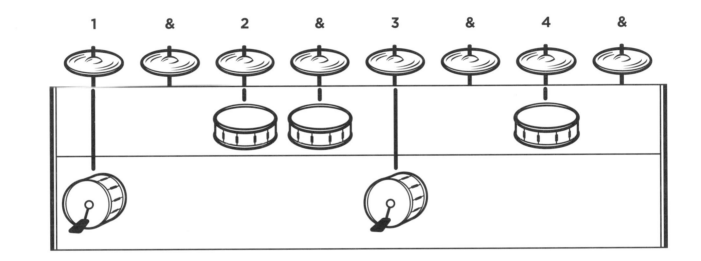

Try practicing beats 24 through 30 with song tracks 53 and 54.

24)

TRACK
30

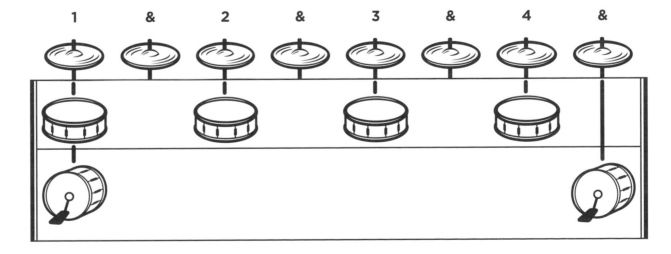

25)

TRACK
31

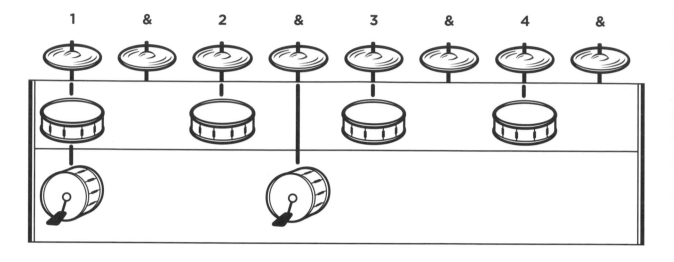

26)

TRACK
32

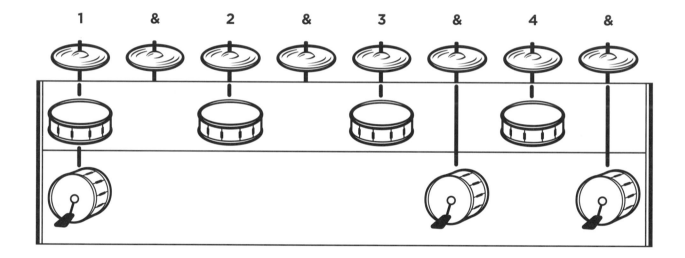

27)

TRACK
33

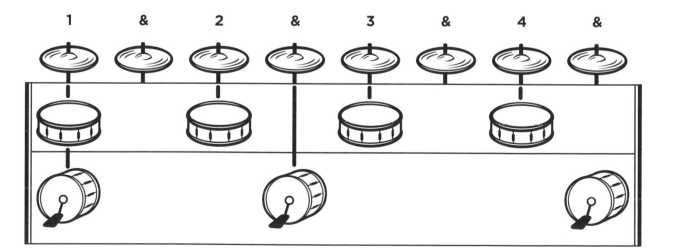

22)

28)

TRACK 34

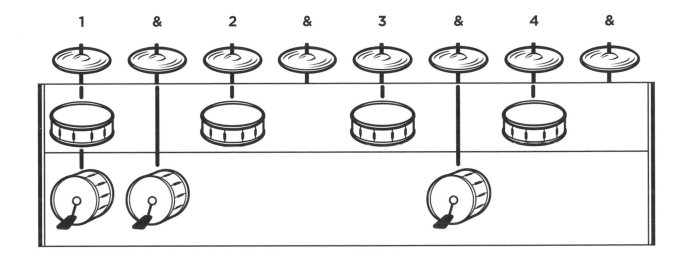

29)

TRACK 35

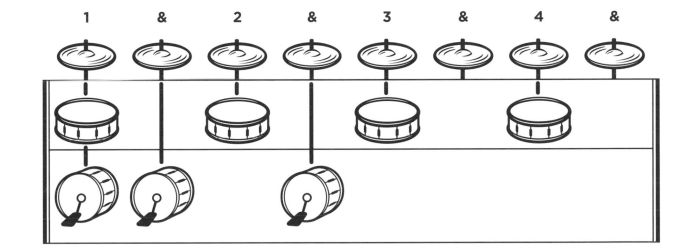

30)

TRACK 36

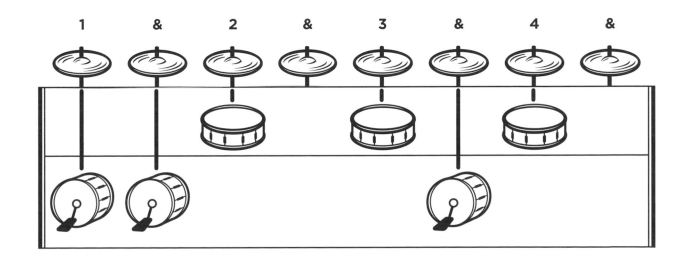

Try practicing beats 31 through 35 with song tracks 55 and 56.

31)

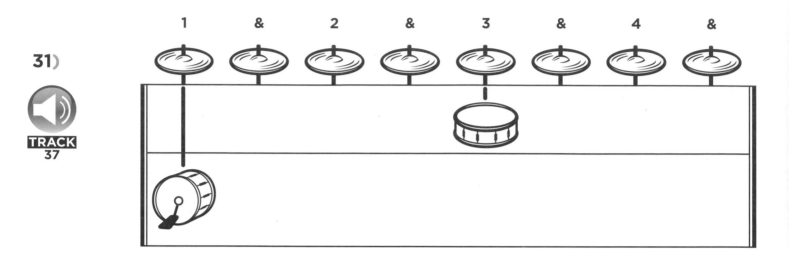

32)

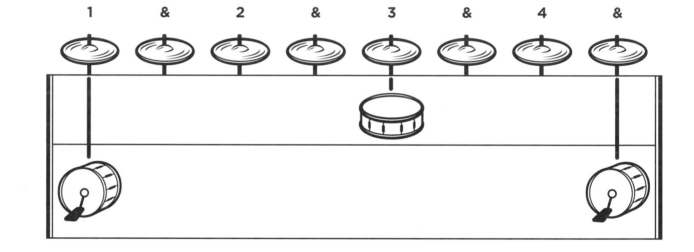

33)

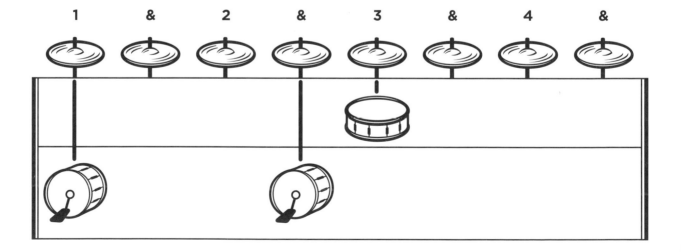

34)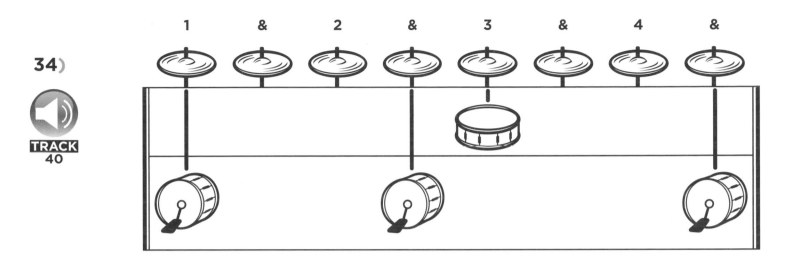

35)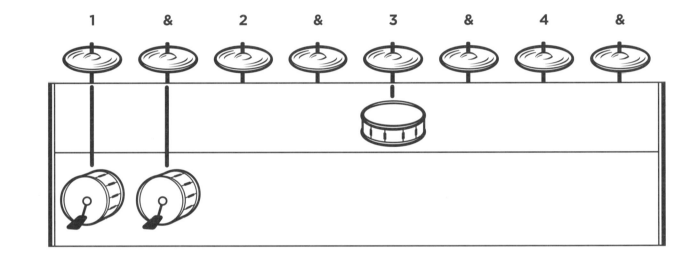

36)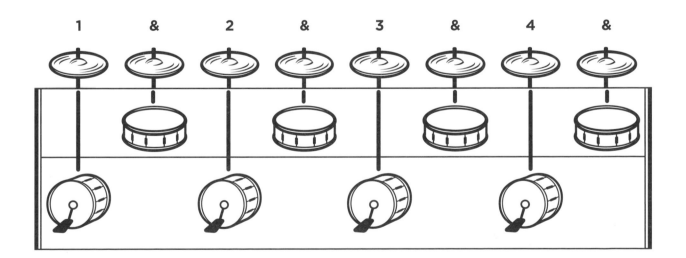

Try practicing beats 37 through 42 with song tracks 57 and 58.

37)

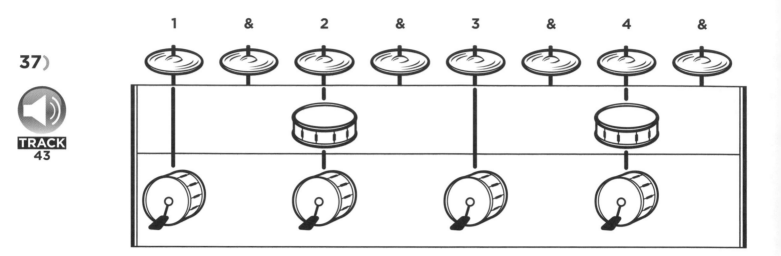

38)

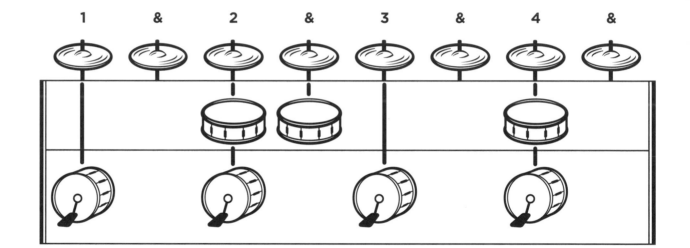

39)

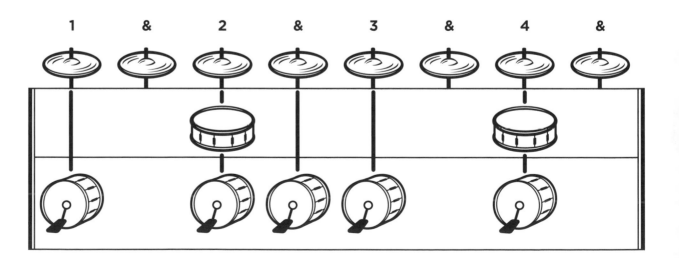

40)

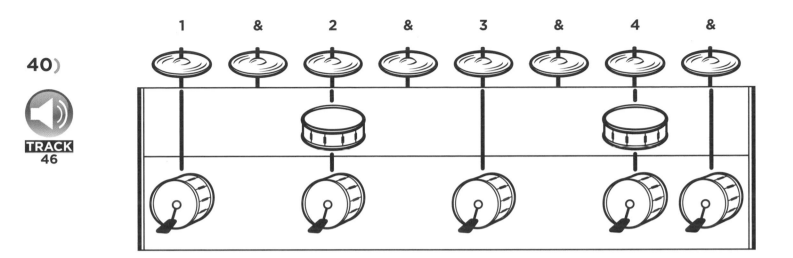

41)

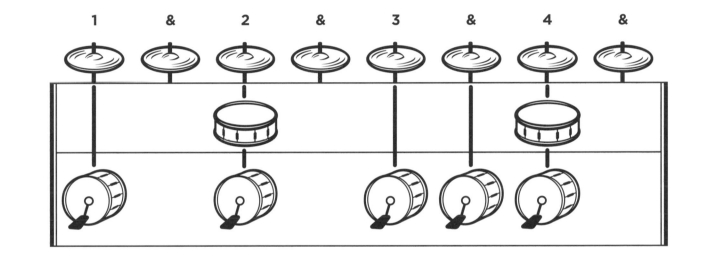

42)

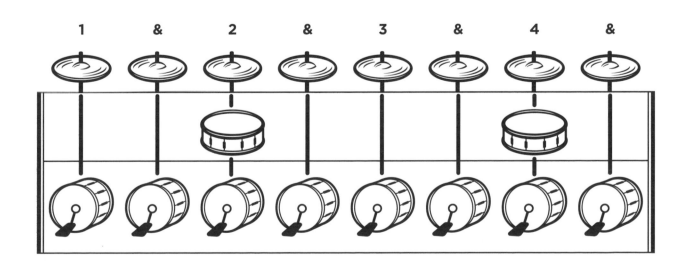

TEACHER'S CHARTS

1)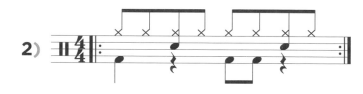

2)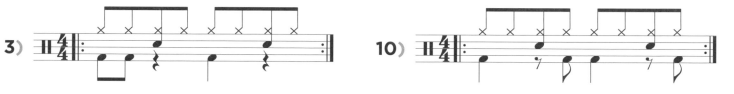

3)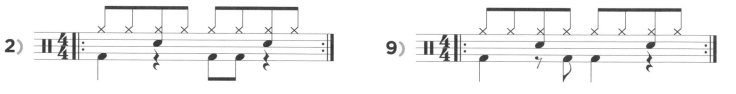

4)

5)

6)

7)

8)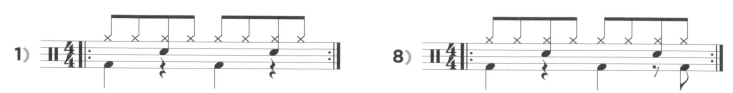

9)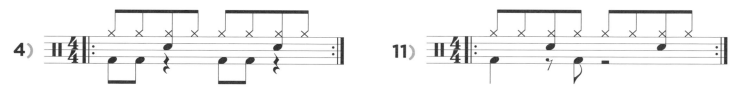

10)

11)

12)

13)

14)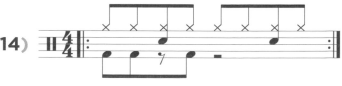

15)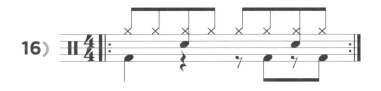

22)

16)

23)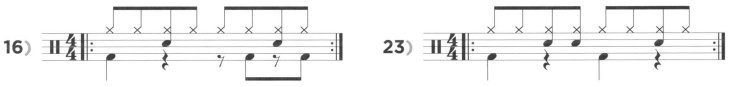

17)

24)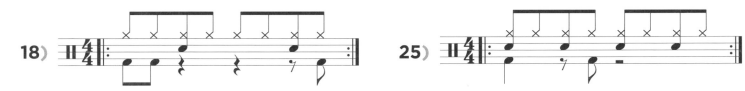

18)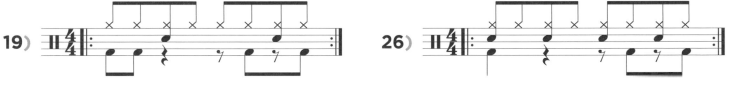

25)

19)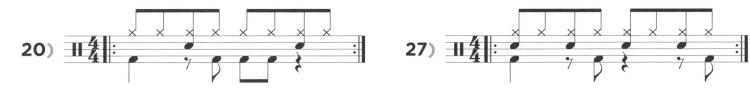

26)

20)

27)

21)

28)

29)

30)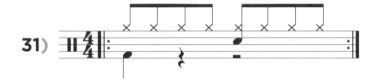

31)

32)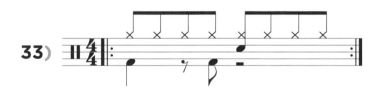

33)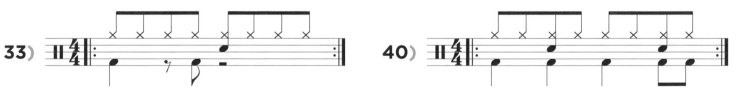

34)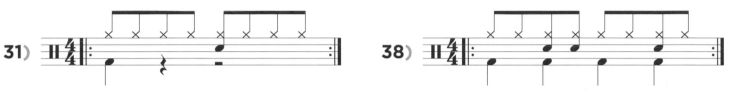

35)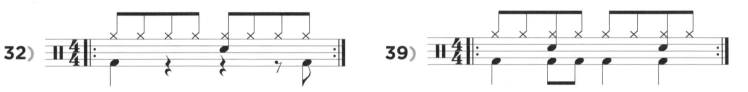

36)

37)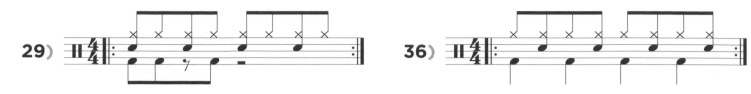

38)

39)

40)

41)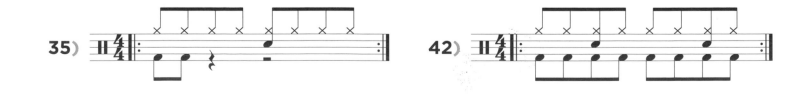

42) (image)

GRAPHIC CUTOUTS

RIGHT HAND

HI-HAT

LEFT HAND

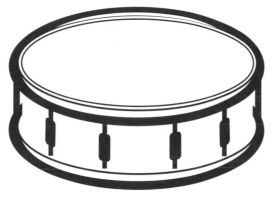

SNARE DRUM

RIGHT FOOT

BASS DRUM